United States
Department of
Agriculture

Forest Service

Pacific Northwest
Research Station

General Technical Report
PNW-GTR-785
April 2009

Cooperative Alaska
Forest Inventory

Thomas Malone, Jingjing Liang, and Edmond C. Packee

Authors

Thomas Malone is a research forester, **Jingjing Liang** is an assistant professor of forest management, and **Edmond C. Packee** is a professor of forest management, emeritus, School of Natural Resources and Agricultural Sciences, University of Alaska Fairbanks, P.O. Box 757200, Fairbanks AK, 99775.

Cover:
Mixed stand of aspen and white spruce, Old Edgerton Highway, Alaska.
Photo by Tom Malone.

Cooperative Alaska Forest Inventory

Thomas Malone, Jingjing Liang, and Edmond C. Packee

Published by:
Boreal Ecology Cooperative Research Unit
Pacific Northwest Research Station
U.S. Department of Agriculture, Forest Service

In cooperation with:
School of Natural Resources and Agricultural Sciences
University of Alaska Fairbanks

Portland, Oregon
General Technical Report PNW-GTR-785
April 2009

Abstract

Malone, Thomas; Liang, Jingjing; Packee, Edmond C. 2009. Cooperative Alaska Forest Inventory. Gen. Tech. Rep. PNW-GTR-785. Portland, OR: U.S. Department of Agriculture, Forest Service, Pacific Northwest Research Station. 42 p.

The Cooperative Alaska Forest Inventory (CAFI) is a comprehensive database of boreal forest conditions and dynamics in Alaska. The CAFI consists of field-gathered information from numerous permanent sample plots distributed across interior and south-central Alaska including the Kenai Peninsula. The CAFI currently has 570 permanent sample plots on 190 sites representing a wide variety of growing conditions. New plots are being added to the inventory annually. To date, over 60 percent of the permanent sample plots have been remeasured and approximately 20 percent have been remeasured three times. Repeated periodic inventories on CAFI permanent sample plots provide valuable long-term information for modeling of forest dynamics such as growth and yield. Periodic remeasurements can also be used to test and monitor large-scale environmental and climate change.

This guide documents sampling and estimation procedures of CAFI v.1.0, and provides details of the database, including attribute description and summary statistics. To help researchers and land managers successfully initiate or expand a permanent sample site program in Alaska, this guide offers a comprehensive tutorial to establish, maintain, and process permanent sample plots in Alaska's boreal forests.

For more information, please visit http://www.faculty.uaf.edu/ffjl2/CAFI.html.

Keywords: CAFI, inventory, forest dynamics, forest health, boreal forest, tree characteristics, basal area, growth, mortality, recruitment, site, soil, ecology.

Contents

Introduction and Background

The boreal forest, the largest forest component of the Alaskan landscape, occupies 60 to 70 percent of Alaska's land area (Van Cleve and Dyrness 1983). The forest consists of eight species dependent upon the taxonomic treatment of the genus *Populus*: three conifers—white spruce (*Picea glauca* (Moench) Voss), black spruce (*Picea mariana* (Mill.) B.S.P.), tamarack (*Larix laricina* (DuRoi) K. Koch)—and five hardwoods—Kenai birch (*Betula kenaica* W.H. Evans), Alaska birch (*Betula neoalaskana* Sarg.), quaking aspen (*Populus tremuloides* Michx.), balsam poplar (*Populus balsamifera* L. spp. *balsamifera*), and western black cottonwood (*Populus balsamifera* L. spp. *trichocarpa* (Torr. & Gray). Of these, white spruce, Alaska birch, Kenai birch, and quaking aspen are currently of significant commercial importance.

The Alaskan boreal forest exists in an environment of extreme climatic conditions that differ considerably across Alaska. For example, in interior Alaska, the difference in temperatures can be as much as 160 °F between summer and winter, and precipitation rarely exceeds 20 in per year. In contrast, in south-central Alaska, the temperature differential between summer and winter is not as extreme, and the heavier snowfall and more rain in south-central Alaska causes different tree growth. Across the full range of the boreal forest in Alaska, the growing season is relatively short compared to other biomes (Van Cleve et al. 1983). However, the long days of the growing season provide more light for photosynthetic activity and thus mitigate, in part, the effect of the short growing season. Despite an increased interest in the resources from these forests, the forest industry in the boreal forest region of Alaska continues to be limited to small mills and cottage industries.

The Cooperative Alaska Forest Inventory (CAFI) is a comprehensive database consisting of field-gathered information on boreal forest conditions and dynamics in Alaska. The overall program was initiated in 1984 by E.C. Packee. Data are collected from sites distributed across interior and south-central Alaska including the Kenai Peninsula (fig. 1).

Permanent sample plots (PSPs) are a valuable tool for resource managers, in part because they provide managers with a wide variety of data and are remeasured periodically. An established PSP database becomes more valuable as the plots are remeasured and maintained over time. A measurement gives a snapshot of the site, but repeated periodic site visits provide much more valuable long-term information on forest growth and yield that aids in the modeling of future forest dynamics. In addition, periodic remeasurement of PSPs across a large area over time can be used to test and monitor large-scale environmental and climate change.

The Cooperative Alaska Forest Inventory (CAFI) is a comprehensive database consisting of field-gathered information on boreal forest conditions and dynamics in Alaska.

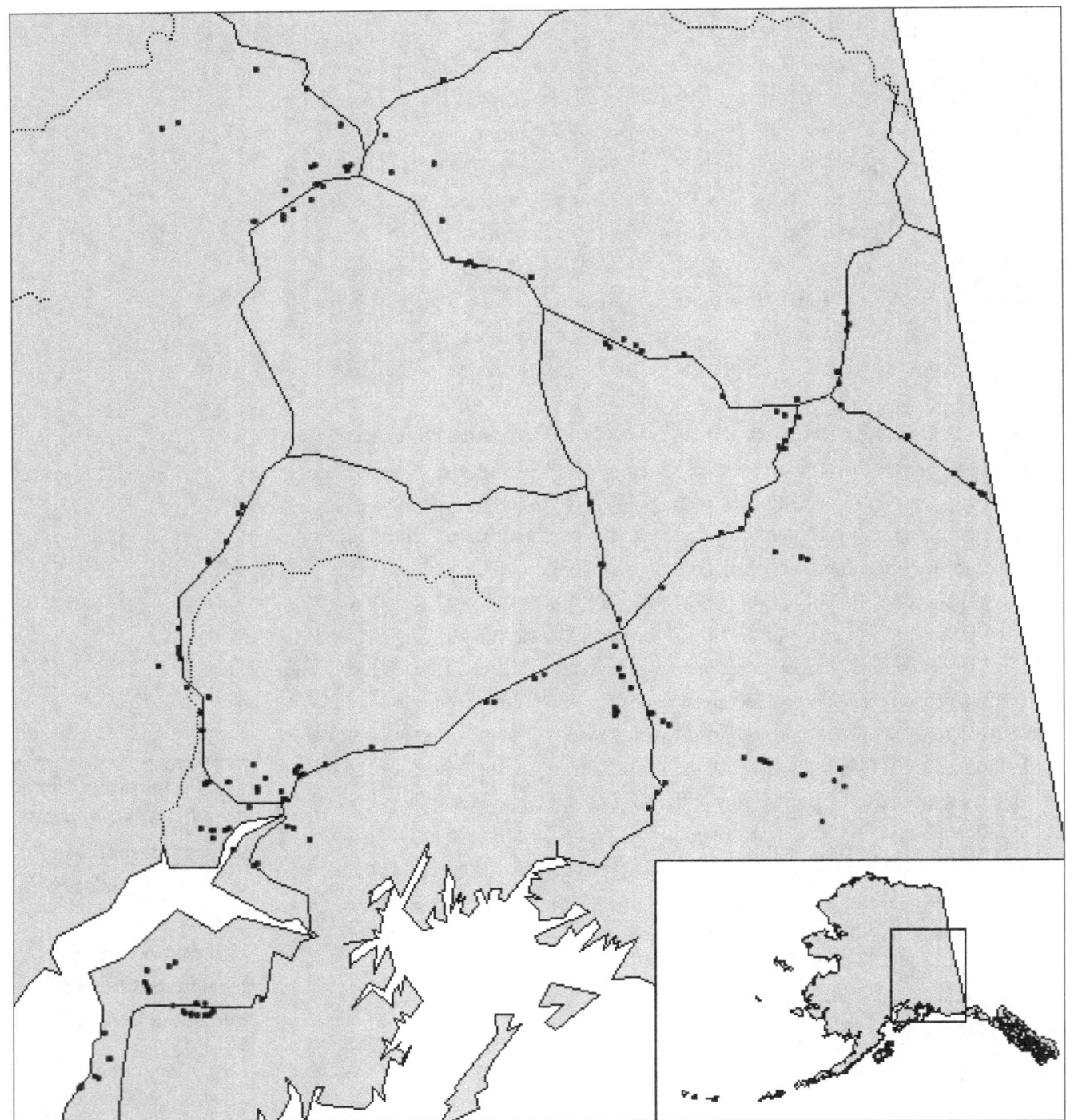

Figure 1—Geographic distribution of the 191 permanent sample plot sites (dots) and their relative location within Alaska (inset). Solid lines represent highways and dotted lines represent major rivers.

This user's guide describes version 1.0 of the CAFI. New data are being continually added to the database; the user's guide will be updated periodically to accommodate future changes. The next sections summarize sampling and estimation procedures for the CAFI and provide details of the database, including attribute descriptions and summary statistics. The appendixes list equipment and supplies used to establish PSPs. The guide also provides detailed procedures to establish, maintain, and process PSPs in Alaska's boreal forests.

For more information on the CAFI, or to request a copy, please visit http://www.faculty.uaf.edu/ffjl2/CAFI.html.

Methods

The CAFI ground plots are a system of fixed-size PSPs, established to monitor growth, yield, and health of boreal forests in Alaska. They cover a large geographic area and multiple ownerships to represent various stand conditions. They have a fixed location and fixed size and are remeasured periodically. Many of the data collection procedures and codes used in this research are taken from General Technical Report PNW-155, *Procedures for establishing and maintaining permanent plots for silivcultural and yield research* (Curtis 1983).

The geographic area includes forested regions dominated by pure or mixed stands of white and black spruce, tamarack, Alaska and Kenai birch, aspen, balsam poplar or, locally, western black cottonwood. Included within the boreal forest are two vegetation types: closed spruce-hardwood forests and open spruce forests (Viereck and Little 1972). On the Kenai Peninsula and in southern south-central Alaska, scattered mountain hemlock (*Tsuga mertensiana* (Bong.) Carr.) and Sitka spruce (*Picea sitchensis* (Bong.) Carr.) may be present as scattered individuals or stands in the transition zone between the boreal forest and the Sitka spruce-western hemlock coastal forest. The boreal forest region is bounded on the north and west by tundra (moist and wet), and shrub land types and on the south by the coastal Sitka spruce-hemlock forests (Viereck and Little 1972).

Site description, tree, and understory vegetation data are collected to quantify site characteristics. Physical site attributes collected include location, slope, aspect, landform, and soils information. Tree data include diameter, height, health, and quality and quantity of regeneration. Presence of understory vegetation, both vascular and nonvascular, is recorded as percentage of cover.

It is important to establish PSPs not only in current forested areas, but also in recently disturbed areas in which forests will become established. In this way, postdisturbance growth rates can be compared to the growth and yield of mature forest stands, and stand development patterns can be observed. Because funding is limited, the only means of transportation for the crews are motor vehicles and walking. To ensure the crews' safety, no PSP site is selected farther than 10 mi from a road. Therefore, all the CAFI PSPs are located within 20-mi corridors surrounding established roads.

The procedure for establishing PSPs is as follows:

1. Prior to sampling at a given location, sites are visually assessed for suitability; this is usually done in spring or summer. To be suitable, a potential PSP site must be in a single forest stand and minimally 5 ac.

2. If the site is deemed suitable, the site location information is brought back to the office for processing a PSP land use permit.

3. Land ownership for each site is determined, and the landowners are contacted to obtain permission to establish a PSP.

4. If the land use is compatible with PSP objectives and will remain that way, and the owner plans to retain the land, a letter is submitted to the landowner requesting permission to establish a PSP. The landowner must grant written permission for a permanent plot to be established and allow the field crew to reenter the land for periodic remeasurement; the landowner will need to be contacted every 5 years. If a public agency manages the land, an appropriate land use permit is necessary; otherwise, a formal letter of permission is adequate.

Field Sampling

Each site consists of three PSPs. Each PSP is located at least 100 ft into a forest stand or potential stand. The closest corner of any of the three PSPs must be at least 100 ft away from openings such as roads, trails, power lines, meadows, or stand openings to avoid an edge effect. The first of the three PSPs is randomly located using the following method: one person stands facing away from the stand, takes a corner post, and throws it back over his head into the stand. The point where the post lands is the first corner of the first PSP from which the rest of the site is established. At each corner and at the PSP center, a 1-ft-long metal post is driven into the ground; thus five posts mark each PSP. Flagging is tied around each corner and the center post so that they can be easily seen. Flagging is also hung in a tree near each post with the PSP number written on it.

The normal layout of the three PSPs at a site is triangular. The second and third PSPs are located 100 ft from the nearest corner of the initial PSP (fig. 2). The second PSP is located on the left side of the initial PSP and the third PSP on the right side at angles of 45° going through the center and either the right or left corner points of the initial PSP. In a rare situation where PSPs cannot be established in the standard triangular layout, other layouts can be employed (fig. 3). In alternate site layouts, the distance between each PSP is still 100 ft.

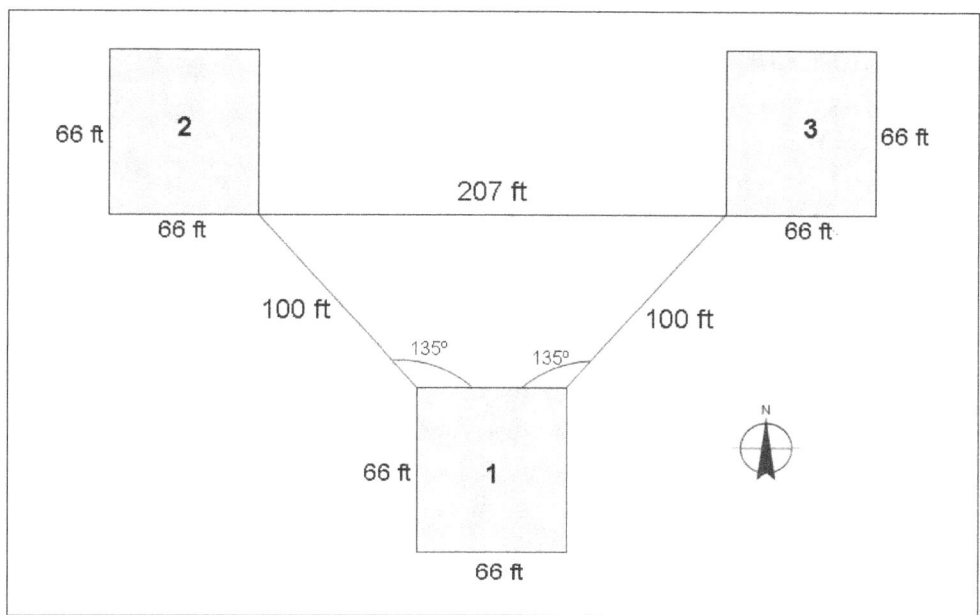

Figure 2—Typical Cooperative Alaska Forest Inventory plot layout within a site.

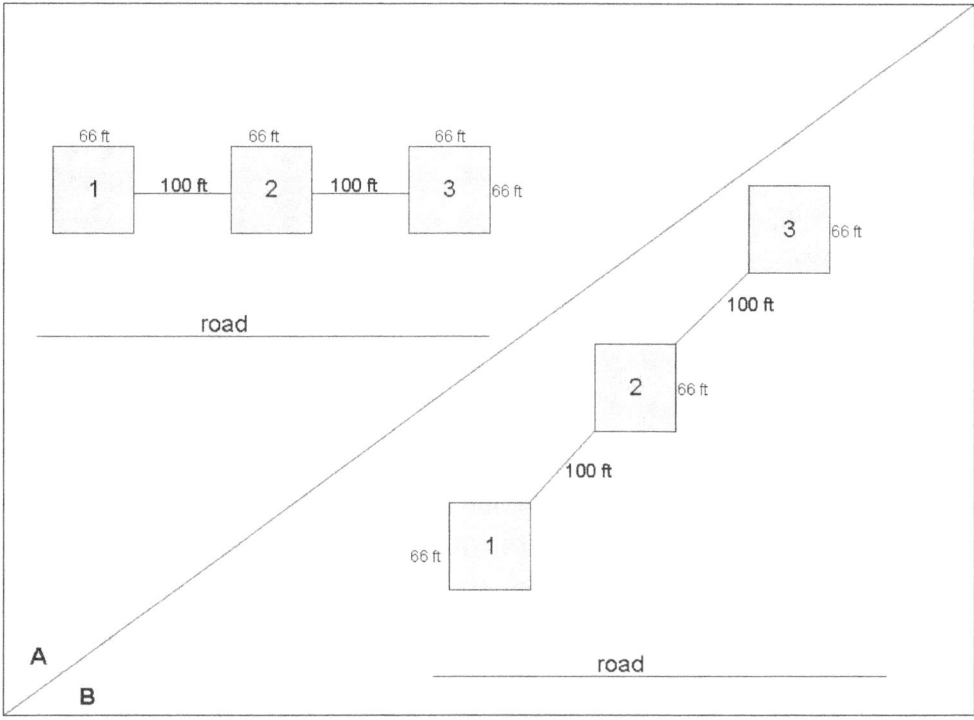

Figure 3—Two alternate Cooperative Alaska Forest Inventory plot layouts.

All PSPs are 0.1 ac and square with 66-ft sides (without regard to slope) (fig. 2). The plots are laid out in the cardinal directions (north, south, east, and west). It is important to ensure that the PSPs are set up as square as possible by using a hand-held compass and tape measure. To improve accuracy, the diagonal is measured and should fall between 91.3 and 95.3 ft.

When revisiting a previously established site, the crew uses a site map and global positioning system (GPS) coordinates to bring the crew to the site and the approximate PSP centers; the previous flagging and corner stakes are used to reestablish plot boundaries. Once all PSPs are relocated, all corners and the center posts and the nearby tree are re-flagged before remeasurement.

Site Data Collection

Land ownership is determined from federal or state status plat maps (U.S. Department of the Interior or State of Alaska); because these are updated periodically, an office visit to the appropriate agency is necessary before remeasurement. The exact legal description of the site is determined and entered into the database after the crew comes back from the field.

The U.S. Public Land Survey System (USPLSS) is used to describe the general location of a PSP site. Data to be entered for each PSP are meridian, township, range, section, and quarter section of the site; this information is obtained from the appropriate U.S. Geological Survey (USGS) quadrant maps. Occasionally, a site is too close to a section line or township line to record the exact legal description from a map. Thus, on site, GPS coordinates are obtained for each PSP and retained in the GPS unit's memory.

The exact center of each PSP is recorded with a GPS unit. The GPS unit is set on the ground on top of the center post to acquire points. A point feature is selected and at least 100 readings are collected to accurately locate the site center. If the satellite signal is weak, it could take up to an hour to acquire at least 100 readings. These readings are then averaged to get accurate coordinates of the PSP center: the latitude, longitude, and elevation. These coordinates are also used to locate the plots for remeasurement.

The GPS coordinates for each of the three PSPs at a site are entered into a mapping program that provides the exact location and the USPLSS description of the PSPs. All the GPS coordinates in CAFI have been rounded up to the nearest 0.01 degree for the purposes of security and privacy.

The following data are collected to complete the site sheet: date; crew members; aspect; slope; presence of permafrost; slope position; contour; bedrock type; landform; soil texture; depth by horizon, color, and moisture; and percentage cover of deadwood, charcoal, mineral soil, litter, snags, trees, and understory vegetation by species.

Aspect identifies the direction of the slope of the PSP, basically which way water runs off the slope. The crew member holds the compass level, points it down slope and records the aspect. If the PSP is flat, aspect is recorded as "0."

Percentage of slope is measured with a clinometer along the same compass bearing as for aspect. A crew person ties flagging, at eye level, to a tree at the lowest point on the PSP boundary and then moves to the highest point and sights on the lower flagging and records the percentage of slope. On variable slopes or where the slope appears flat, several measurements may be needed to get the average slope.

Permafrost is an earth material that has had a temperature below 32 °F for 2 years or more. The presence of permafrost can be determined by observation of a soil pit, landscape position, and/or using vegetation as an indicator. Three basic classes of permafrost exist across the Alaska boreal forest landscape: continuous permafrost occurs north of the Brooks Range and in western interior Alaska, discontinuous permafrost occurs in central and eastern interior Alaska and in the Copper River basin, and sporadic permafrost occurs in south-central Alaska. Permafrost on the Kenai Peninsula is extremely rare.

To determine bedrock types, we observe parent materials on or below the surface either in or near the sites. A USGS soil survey can also be used to determine bedrock type.

Landform is the name for the physical process that formed the topographic features within the PSP. Soil types and formation observed in a soil pit can assist in determining landform. Local soil survey maps and surface deposit maps and reports can also assist in determining landform.

Soil characteristics (Schoeneberger et al. 2002) are recorded for each PSP and are derived from a soil pit dug outside the PSP near the northwest corner. Soil pits are dug to the depth of 39 in or to parent material, whichever comes first. In most cases, mineral soil is found below the surface organic horizons. In some cases, this organic horizon can extend much deeper than 39 in.

Soil Texture is the size and quantity of particles in the mineral soil layer as detected by touch. Texture is an estimate of the relative proportions of sand, silt, and clay particles. Soil texture follows the NRCS definitions of soil particles.

Organic Depth includes all surface organic horizons in the soil pit. The surface organic horizons consist of fresh and well-decayed plant and animal litter. Measurement is total thickness of organic matter from the bottom of the live/green vegetation to the top of the underlying mineral horizons. Organic depth ranges from 0 to more than 39 in.

The Oi horizon is the uppermost organic horizon, also referred to as the L horizon. The Oi horizon consists of undecayed to slightly decayed plant material; leaves, needles, twigs, and roots are still recognizable. Thickness is measured, in inches, from the top of the litter to the top of the Oe, Oa, or mineral horizon.

The Oe horizon if present, is below the Oi horizon. This horizon is referred to as the F horizon. The Oe horizon consists of partially decayed plant material with little if any in its original condition; 7 to 75 percent is still fibrous after being rubbed between the fingers. Thickness is measured, in inches, from the bottom of the Oi horizon to the top of the Oa or mineral horizon.

The Oa horizon if present, is below the Oe or Oi horizon. It is referred to as the H horizon. The Oa horizon consists of well-decayed plant material with little if any in its original or fibrous condition; it is <7 percent fibrous by volume and has a greasy feel and tends to stain fingers. Thickness is measured, in inches, from the bottom of the Oe or Oi horizon to the top of the mineral horizon.

The mineral layer is measured from the bottom of the organic horizon, if present, to parent material or 39 in, whichever comes first. For measurement purposes, parent material (bedrock) begins where the shovel hits mostly broken-up rock fragments with little fine-grained material.

Soil color is the color of mineral soil in the soil pit and can be determined from the same soil sample used to identify soil texture. The color must be determined immediately after the soil is excavated from the pit. There can be numerous color horizons within a single soil pit. Color identification consists of three notations: hue, value, and chroma as defined in the Munsell soil color chart (Macbeth 2000) and in the glossary.

Soil moisture reflects the general soil drainage conditions in each PSP as observed in the amount of water in the soil. Observation of other conditions can help determine soil moisture, such as wet shoes from working on the site, or a south-facing sparse aspen stand.

Cover class is a measure used to quantify the remaining attributes in the site table. To determine the cover class, the recorder imagines that they are looking down on the PSP from above and estimates the percentage of the PSP that is covered by each attribute.

To ensure that all the attributes are accurately estimated, a crew member must walk through the 0.1-ac PSP several times, and the most accurate and efficient way to walk through the PSP is in a systematic pattern. Start in the northwest corner and walk to the northeast corner and then to the southeast corner, then to the southwest corner and finally back to the northwest corner. The recorder then moves into the plot a few feet and repeats the forgoing square pattern spiraling inward until arriving at the center. At this time, the recorder has observed the PSP characteristics and can assign a cover class to the appropriate site attributes.

Dead wood includes branches and twigs larger than 1 inch in diameter lying on the ground, standing dead tree less than 4.5 in high, and other dead woody plants such as alder.

Charcoal includes burned wood observed in the soil pit as well as burned wood remaining on surface of site.

Mineral soil exposed includes soil exposed on a steep slope, by uprooted trees, or by various disturbances such as fire or flood.

Litter includes nonliving vegetative material such as dead leaves, cones, stems, and twigs smaller than 1 inch in diameter.

Snags are dead standing trees at least 4.5 ft tall.

Tree cover is percentage of plot covered by numbered trees in the PSP.

Understory vegetation includes all tree regeneration, shrubs, herbs, moss, lichen, and grass. The first three letters of the genus and the first three letters of the species are recorded for each species along with the percentage cover class.

At least four pictures are taken from the northwest corner of each PSP during site establishment and subsequent remeasurements. The first picture is taken of a paper with the PSP number and current year written on it. The second picture is taken with the camera pointed toward the northeast corner. The third picture is taken with the camera pointed at PSP center. The fourth picture is taken with the camera pointed at the southwest corner. Additional pictures can be taken of unique features within or near the PSP.

Tree Data Collection

The CAFI tree data collection follows the procedures below:
1. Number the trees in the PSP.
2. Measure diameter at breast height (d.b.h.) and paint a d.b.h. band on each tree.
3. Assess the health of that tree.
4. Measure tree height and length of live crown.

Trees are numbered in a boustrophedonic (alternating direction) order starting in the northwest corner and moving toward the northeast corner of each PSP (fig. 4). Number tags are pinned into the ground on the east side of each tree. Trees in a PSP should be consecutively numbered in the proper order to make it easier to locate them in the future, and no number should be repeated in a site. In the CAFI, tall shrubs are not considered trees. Trees less than 4.5 ft in height or less than 0.51 in d.b.h. are not tagged or measured.

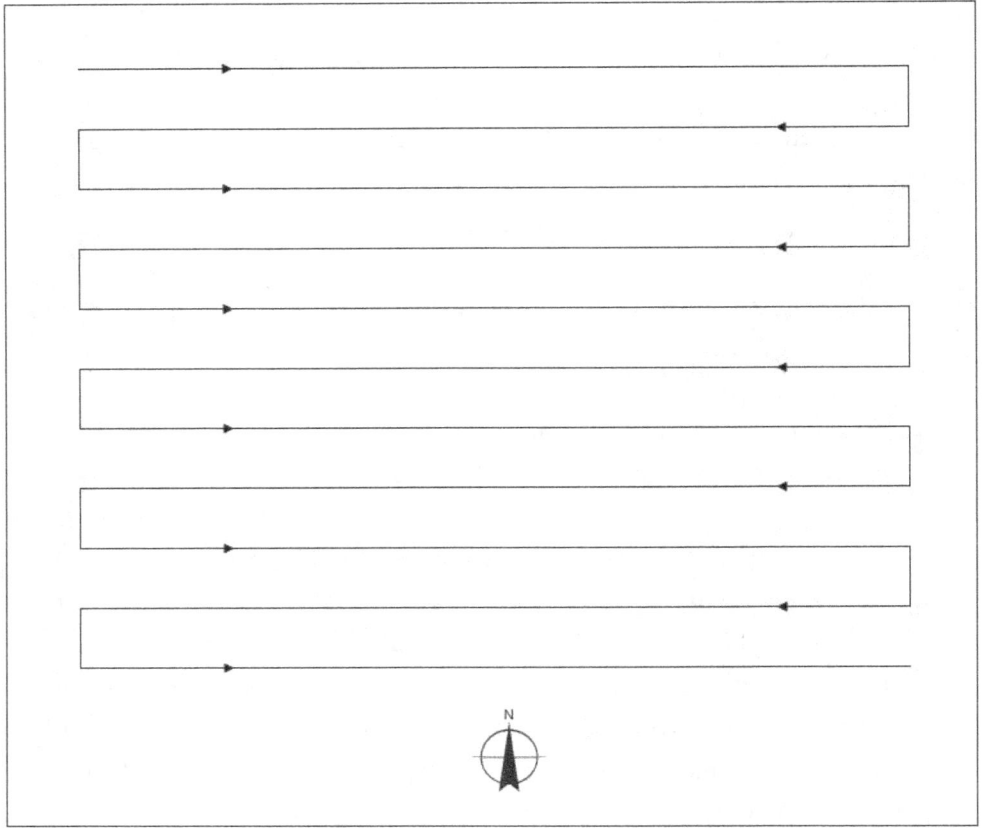

Figure 4—Order of tree numbering beginning in the northwest corner.

Trees on the line, either in or out of the PSP, need to be treated consistently. A borderline tree is determined based on the location of the center of the tree at ground level. Trees with their base more than halfway in the PSP are considered in the PSP. Trees that fall exactly halfway in and halfway out of the PSP are alternately counted as "in" or "out."

In the field, tree data are also entered into a hand-held field computer. A tree data template is preloaded into a spreadsheet (fig. 5). All data recorded into the spreadsheet are in numeric codes or actual measurements. After returning from the field, all the data stored in the field computer are checked and transferred to the TREE_INVENTORY tables.

Tree Number	Species (code)	DBH inch	Total Ht. 1.0 feet	Crown Ht. 1.0 feet	Crown Class	Status Code	Location	Severity	General	Specific	Location	Severity	General	Specific	Location
643	4					2									
644	4	7.07			2		8	3	2	5	5	3	3	2	
645	4	8.35	62	15	2		5	1	3	8					
646	5	6.92	46	24	3		8	1	2	5					
647	5	3.03	30	22	5										
648	5	9.08	57	40	3		2	3	3	5					
649	4	6.12	53	3	3		5	2	3	8	8	1	2	5	5
650	4					2									
651	4	9.76	66	26	2										
652	4	6.67			3		8	3	2	5					
653	5	7.32	32	16	3		2	3	3	5	6	1	3	2	
654	5	2.89			5		6	1	3	2	2	3	2	5	
655	5	8.53	47	35	3		3	1	5	5	8	1	2	5	
656	5	5.6	40	24	3		8	1	2	5	5	1	3	4	3
657	5	12.31	77	52	1										
658	5	3.25	26	12	3		8	1	2	5	2	3	3	5	
659	4	8.3			2		8	2	2	5	5	3	3	2	
660	5	10.32	69	48	1		3	1	5	5					
661	4	5.52	48	15	3		8	3	2	5	5	1	3	2	
662	4	9.87	63	22	2		2	1	2	5					
663	4					2									
664	4	5.58	55	14	3		8	2	2	5					
665	5	3.55	40	25	3		2	1	3	2					
666	5	2.51	32	12	3										
667	5	3.74	33	20	3		3	1	5	5					
668	5	2.57	26	14	5		5	1	3	8	6	1	3	8	2
669	4	5.6			3		8	3	2	5	5	3	3	2	
670	4	7.25	54	20	2		8	2	2	5	5	3	3	4	
671	5	3.12	26	12	5		2	3	3	2	5	1	3	2	
672	5	7.93	58	34	2		5	1	3	4	3	2	5	5	
673	5	12.78	76	46	1		3	2	5	5					
674	5	11.82	76	58	1		8	1	2	5	5	1	3	4	3
675	5	4.82	26	11	5		8	2	2	5	2	3	3	5	
676	5	12.07	71	49	2		3	2	5	5					

LOCATION: PARKS HWY 343.3 MI
PLOT NUMBER: 24
PLOT SHAPE: Square
PLOT SIZE: 0.1 acre
CREW: JG KC SP
DATE: 6 JULY 2005

Figure 5—Example of tree data in a spreadsheet.

Diameter at breast height—

The diameter of each tagged tree is measured at breast height (4.5 ft) (see fig. 6). Tree records are measured to the nearest 0.01 in. A band of red paint is applied around the bole with a paint stick at the place where the diameter measurement is taken. Figure 6 illustrates various deviations from a diameter measurement:

- If a tree is growing on a slope, the measurement is taken on the high (uphill) side of the tree at 4.5 ft above the ground (fig. 6b).

- If a tree is leaning, the measurement is taken on the up side of the tree (fig. 6c).

- If the stem of a tree is forked below breast height, each stem is treated as a separate tree (fig. 6d). Therefore, two numbered tags are placed at the base of the stem. They are both measured and recorded separately.

- If a tree has deformity on the bole at breast height that prevents an accurate or representative diameter measurement, the measurement is taken above or below the deformity where the bole resumes a "normal" taper (fig. 6e).

- Finally, if two stems have grown too close together to fit a tape measure between the stems, each stem is treated as a separate tree. Diameter is measured with a caliper, or a mark is placed halfway around the stem and a radial measurement is taken and multiplied by two for a diameter determination (fig. 6f).

The diameter is recorded to the nearest 0.01 inch in column C. If the tree is a young conifer, it may not be possible to take an accurate diameter measurement because of guard hairs (needles) surrounding the stem.

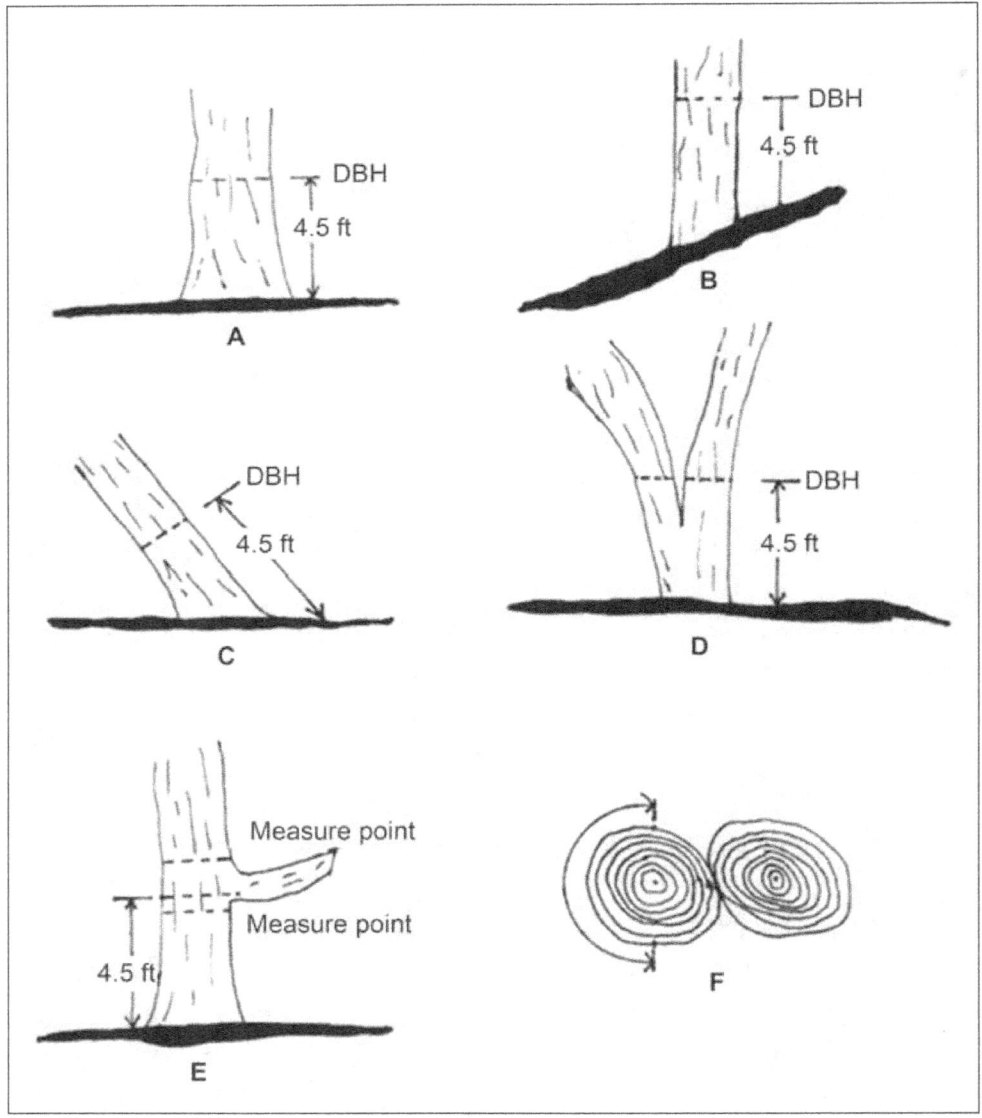

Figure 6—Methods for measuring diameter at breast height (DBH). when (a) the tree is on level ground, (b) the tree is on a slope, (c) the tree is leaning, (d) the tree is forked below breast height, (e) the tree has an irregular bole at breast height, and (f) tree boles touch at breast height.

The crown class of each tree is entered in column F. Trees within a PSP are coded as either dominant, codominant, intermediate, suppressed, understory, or overstory.

Tree status and visual defects—

Tree status category lists a wide variety of tree conditions from live to dead to having a missing numbered tag from previous inventories. It also allows notation that a current inventory measurement is correct and a previous measurement was incorrect. The remaining 16 columns, H through W, in the tree data (fig. 5) identify visual defects on the tree for up to four damages. The damage is identified by its location on the tree (top, limbs, foliage, bole, base, or roots), the severity, and the general and specific type of visual damage. This code classification is broken down into two parts: the general classification includes crown disease, bole disease, insects, and weather; the specific damage code includes spruce needle cast, fluting, ants, and winter burn. For example, the damage/defect code of a tree that is forked at the base would be 6332 (bole defect, severe damage, bole disease or abnormality, multiple stems or forks).

Tree height—

Total tree height and live crown length are measured with a hypsometer (fig. 7) and recorded into the tree data template in columns D and E. There are numerous types of hypsometers such as a Biltmore stick, an Abney level, clinometer, relascope, and a laser hypsometer. Currently, the most accurate, fastest, and easiest instrument with which to measure heights is a laser hypsometer such as an Impulse 200[1] laser hypsometer.

In an area such as an open stand where there is no obstruction between the laser instrument and the target tree, the distance measurement can be shot directly from the bole of the tree to the laser instrument. In most forested stands, however, there are too many obstructions for a laser beam to strike the target tree bole directly. The laser could hit a branch or leaf and give a false distance reading. In this case, the filter mode must be selected in the Impulse laser. To acquire an accurate distance measurement in the filter mode, a laser reflector must be placed at the bole of the tree. The first measurement of distance is shot at the laser reflector (fig. 7, measurement 1). The person that is measuring diameter can hold up a laser reflector for the person measuring height. The measurements taken at the base and top are angle measurements and do not need to strike a laser reflector. In forested stands,

---

[1] The use of trade or firm names in this publication is for reader information and does not imply endorsement by the U.S. Department of Agriculture or the University of Alaska of any product or service.

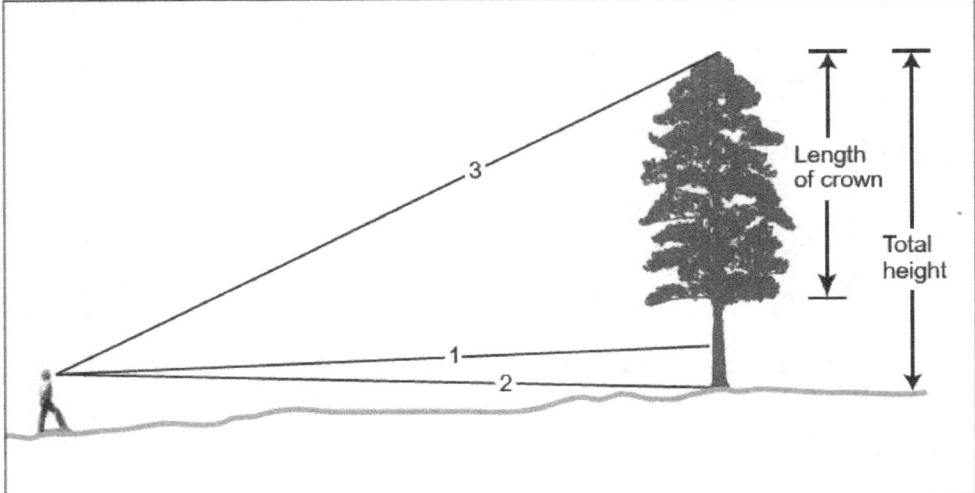

Figure 7—Tree height measurements where measurement 1 is the distance between the operator and the target tree, measurement 2 is the distance between the operator and the ground at the base of the target tree, and measurement 3 is the distance between the operator and the top of the target tree.

where the laser operator must stand a long distance from the target tree, it is often necessary for someone to shake the tree so the correct tree top can be identified and measured.

Crown class and length—
Crown class is the relative position of the tree crown with respect to the competing vegetation around it. Crown class for each tree is judged visually in the context of its immediate environment, which includes trees or shrubs competing for sunlight with the subject tree. In the CAFI, crown class categories include dominant, codominant, intermediate, suppressed, overstory, and understory.

The live crown starts at a point where the first continuous live crown branches protrude from the bole, without regard for branch droop. Epicormic branching low on a bole is not considered part of the continuous live crown. To acquire the length of live crown, the Impulse 200 is pointed at the bottom of the live crown to obtain the distance from the base of the tree to the bottom of the live crown. This distance is then subtracted from the total tree height to determine the length of live crown.

Database Structure and Description

The CAFI database is composed of key tables and description tables stored in a single Microsoft® Office Access 2003 database. The current version of the database (CAFI 1.0) has four key tables: SITE, TREE_INVENTORY_1, TREE_INVENTORY_2, and TREE_INVENTORY_3. The definition of each coded variable was provided by the description tables in the same database.

The table provides detailed site-level records, including the location, geographic features, site characteristics, and crew records. TREE_INVENTORY_n provides tree-level records of the nth inventory (e.g., TREE_INVENTORY_1 contains tree records of the first inventory). All the key tables are related by the PSP identification numbers (PSP and TREE-ID, respectively) (fig. 8) so that users can relate tree records to the characteristics of the site that these trees grow on.

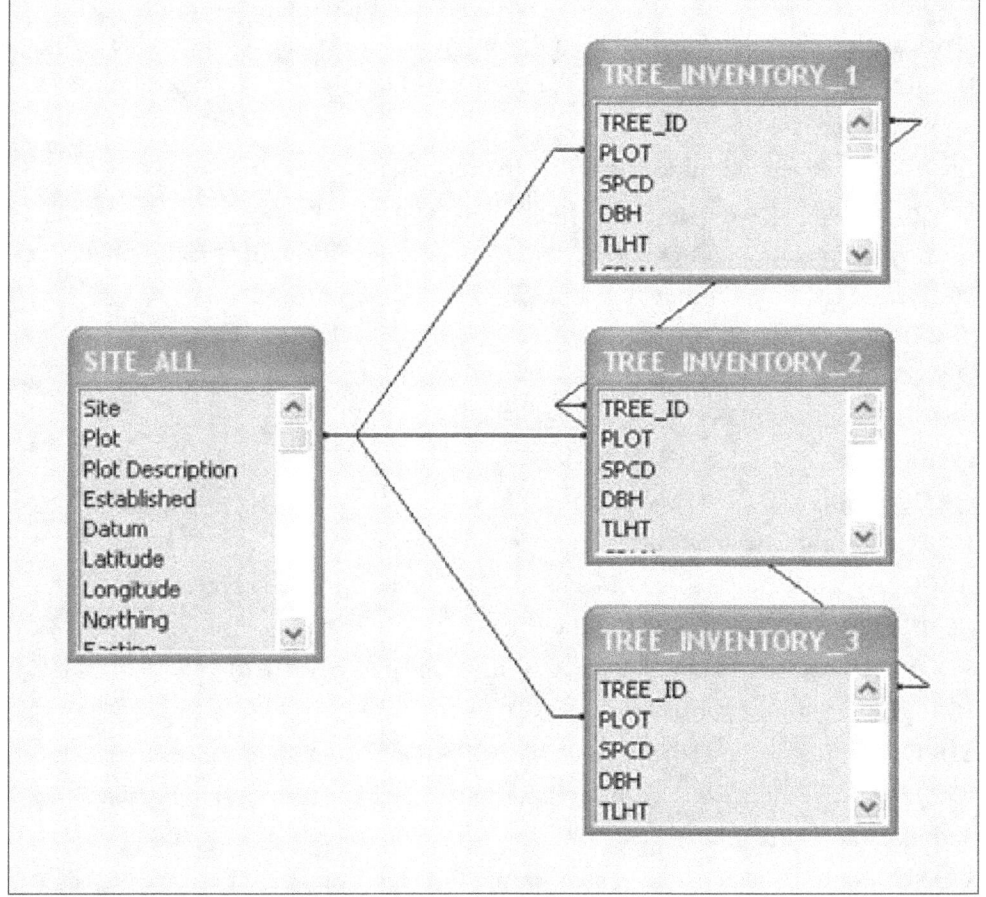

Figure 8—Relationships among the key tables.

The following sections give detailed description of site and tree records and summary statistics of all the measurements. For each coded attribute, there is a table explaining the description of all the classes.

Site Records

There are 37 site attributes. Their name, data type, and unit are listed in table 1. The detailed description is given below:

Site: A unique sequential number used to identify each site.

PSP: A unique sequential number used to identify each 0.1-ac PSP.

Site description: A short paragraph describing location and other unique features of the site.

Established: Month, day, and year of the site establishment.

Ownership: Landowner and/or manager of the site area (coded list in table 2).

Datum: Set of reference points on the Earth's surface against which position measurements are made.

Latitude: Geodetic latitude of the PSP in decimal degrees.

Longitude: Geodetic longitude of the PSP in decimal degrees.

Elevation: Elevation of the PSP in feet obtained from GPS unit or USGS map.

MERI: USGS code for mapping Alaska.

TWSP: Township (USGS code).

RANG: Range (USGS code).

SECT: Section (USGS code).

QTSC: Quarter section (USGS code).

CREW: Initials of each crew member.

DATE: Month, day, and year of the current inventory.

ASPC: Aspect as measured with a hand-held compass to the nearest degree (1° to 360°). A zero is recorded if the PSP is flat.

SLOP: Percentage of slope as measured to the nearest percent (0 to 90 percent).

PERM: Presence of permafrost (table 3).

SLPO: Slope position is the position of the PSP in relation to the surrounding topography as determined by observation. See a detailed description in table 4 and illustration in fig. 9.

CONT: Contour shape is the general form of the land surface within the PSP as determined by observation. See a detailed description in table 5.

BDRK: Presence or absence of bedrock on or beneath the PSP. Observe parent material on or below the surface either in or near the site (table 6).

LNFM: Landform (table 7).

SOTXI and SOTXII: Soil texture for mineral soil layers 1 and 2, respectively (table 8).

SOOR: Thickness of all surface organic horizons in inches.

SOOi: Thickness of the Oi horizon in inches.

SOOe: Thickness of the Oe horizon, if present.

SOOa: Thickness of the Oa horizon, if present.

SOMD: Depth of mineral soil to nearest 0.1 in.

SOCI and SOCII: Color of the first and second mineral soil horizons.

SOMO: General soil drainage conditions (table 9).

DDWD: Percentage of dead wood cover (table 10).

CHAR: Percentage of the PSP covered with charcoal (table 10).

MNSO: Percentage of PSP with mineral soil exposed (table 10).

LTER: Percentage of PSP covered with litter (table 10).

SNAG: Number of snags on the PSP.

Table 1—Permanent sample plots site and plot attributes

Attribute	Full name	Data type	Value or unit
Site	Site number	Integer	Number
PSP	PSP number	Integer	Number
Site description	Site description	Character	Description
Established	Date of establishment	Date	MM/DD/YYYY
Ownership	Landowner/manager	Character	Code
Datum	Datum	WGS84	Code
Latitude	Latitude of the PSP	Real number	Decimal degrees
Longitude	Longitude of the PSP	Real number	Decimal degrees
Elevation	PSP elevation	Real number	Feet
MERI	Meridian	Character	Coded
TWSP	Township	Character	Coded
RANG	Range	Character	Coded
SECT	Section	Integer	Coded
QTSC	Quarter section	Character	Two letters
CREW	Crew names, current inventory	Character	Name
DATE	Current inventory date	Date	MM/DD/YYYY
ASPC	Aspect	Real number	Degrees
SLOP	Slope	Real number	Percent
PERM	Permafrost	Integer	Coded
SLPO	Slope position	Integer	Coded
CONT	Contour	Integer	Coded
BDRK	Bedrock	Integer	Coded
LNFM	Landform	Integer	Coded
SOTXI	Soil texture 1	Integer	Coded
SOTXII	Soil texture 2	Integer	Coded
SOOR	Organic horizon thickness	Real number	Inches
SOOi	Thickness Oi (L)	Real number	Inches
SOOe	Thickness Oe (F)	Real number	Inches
SOOa	Thickness Oa (H)	Real number	Inches
SOMD	Thickness of mineral soil	Real number	Inches
SOCI	Soil color 1	Character	Coded
SOCII	Soil color 2	Character	Coded
SOMO	Soil moisture regime	Integer	Coded
DDWD	Deadwood current inventory	Integer	Coded
CHAR	Charcoal current inventory	Integer	Coded
MNSO	Mineral soil current inventory	Integer	Coded
LTER	Litter current inventory	Integer	Coded
SNAG	Number of snags current inventory	Integer	Number

Table 2—Land ownership description

Class	Description
STATE	Alaska Department of Natural Resources Division of Lands
STATEP	Alaska Department of Natural Resources Division of Parks
STATEM	Alaska Mental Health Trust Lands
STATEF	Alaska Department of Fish and Game
FNSB	Fairbanks North Star Borough
KPB	Kenai Peninsula Borough
MSB	Matanuska Susitna Borough
AHTNA	Ahtna Regional Native Corporation
CIRI	Cook Inlet Regional Native Corporation
DLVC	Dot Lake Village Corporation
NVC	Northway Village Corporation
UA	University of Alaska Statewide Land Management
UAAFES	University of Alaska Agricultural and Forestry Experiment Station
DODA	U.S. Department of Defense, Army
DODAF	U.S. Department of Defense, Air Force
BLM	U.S. Department of the Interior, Bureau of Land Management
KNWR	U.S. Department of the Interior, Fish and Wildlife Service, Kenai National Wildlife Refuge
WSENP	U.S. Department of the Interior, National Park Service, Wrangell St. Elias National Park

Table 3—Permafrost classification

Code	Class	Description
1	Near surface	Permafrost obviously present. It is near the surface, within 2 ft, and is usually ice rich. In these situations the permafrost forms an impermeable layer blocking drainage. The soil is usually saturated near the surface and has a thick organic horizon. Tree growth is commonly stunted.
2	Probably	The active layer is thick (>3 ft) or there is not much ice present, permafrost may not be conclusively evident but some evidence suggests it is present. This may occur in better drained north-facing stony soils or in transition zones. Items to look for are thermokarst activity such as pits and tilting trees, or depressed growth rates of trees. Sites that are northeast- or northwest-facing are suspect. Upland slopes that have near saturated soils are suspect.
3	Probably not	No real strong evidence indicates permafrost presence on this plot. The sites may be flat or near the lower portions of south-facing slopes or along the flood plain where the trees show vigorous growth. This situation may arise when a site obviously had permafrost at one time but the vegetation has been cleared so that the permafrost has melted to some depth.
4	None	Warm, well to moderately well-drained sites on south-facing slopes and along active river channels.
5	Unknown	

Table 4—Slope position

Code	Class	Description
1	Crest	The generally convex uppermost portion of a hill. It is usually convex in all directions. No distinct aspect. A moisture-shedding site
2	Upper slope	The generally upper portion of the slope of a hill. It has a convex surface profile with a specific aspect. It is a moisture-receiving and -shedding site
3	Mid slope	The area of the slope between the upper slope and the lower slope. The general profile is neither concave nor convex; it has a straight or undulating surface profile with a specific aspect. A moisture-receiving and -shedding site.
4	Lower slope	The area near the base of the slope of the hill; where the percentage of slope lessens. It generally has a concave surface profile with a specific aspect. It is a moisture-receiving site.
5	Toe	The lower part of the slope with greatly reduced percentage of slope. It may be demarcated by an abrupt leveling of slope and change in vegetation. Moisture-receiving site, often characterized by seepage.
6	Depression	Area concave in all directions. Typically flat or gently sloping topography. Normally, a poorly drained site, receiving moisture and possibly wet.
7	Stream bottom	Area near an active waterway characterized by level surface or slight slope toward stream. Surface and soil moisture controlled by fluvial activity.
8	Bench/flat	Area more-or-less level and not directly influenced by adjacent topography. Little or no aspect. Moisture is from precipitation.

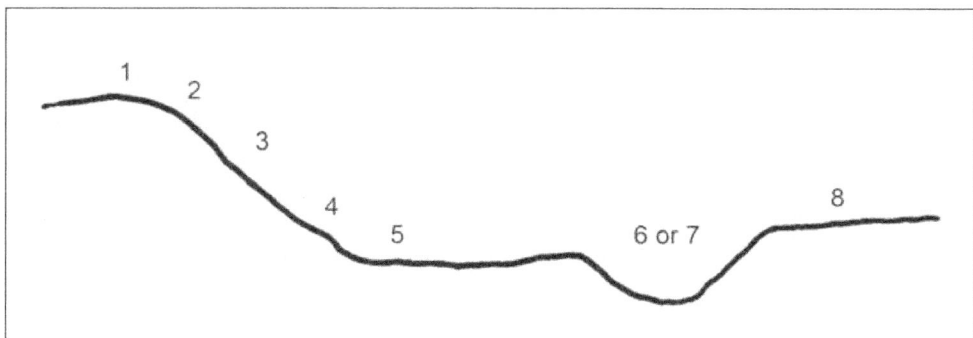

Figure 9—Slope position code in relation to the surrounding topography (see detailed description in table 4).

Table 5—Contour types

Code	Class	Description
1	Convex	Surface curved upward like the top half of a sphere.
2	Straight	Surface generally free of curves, bends, and irregularities.
3	Concave	Surface that is curved inward like the inside of a bowl.
4	Undulating	Surface wavy; landscape fluctuates with rises and falls.

Table 6—Bedrock types

Code	Class	Description
1	Igneous	Igneous rock is formed by solidification from a molten or partially molten state. This designation involves both the deep-seated plutonic igneous rocks as well as the shallow intrusive and volcanic or extrusive igneous rocks.
2	Metamorphic	Metamorphic rocks are those formed by the alteration in composition, texture, or internal structure of preexisting consolidated rocks subjected to heat, pressure, and the introduction of new chemical substances.
3	Sedimentary	Sedimentary rocks are formed by the accumulation of sediment in water or from air. The sediments may consist of detrital fragments of various-sized (conglomerate, sandstone, siltstone, shale) remains of products of plants or animals (coal, limestone), chemical action (precipitation), or evaporation (salt, gypsum, some carbonate rocks) or combinations of these minerals/ processes.
4	None	Indeterminable.

Table 7—Landforms

Code	Class	Description
1	Colluvial	Material moved downslope chiefly by gravity. Composition of deposits vary widely. Avalanche, rock glaciers, landside, mudflow, solifluction, and talus.
2	Aeolian	Deposits consist of silt and fine sand eroded, transported, and then deposited by wind action. Loess deposits in interior Alaska, sand dunes.
3	Flood plain (active)	Deposits consist of sediments transported and deposited by flowing rivers and streams. Generally fine-grained cover deposits laid down above the riverbed deposits during bank overflow. Usually an active flood plain is permafrost free and has groundwater moving through. It is adjacent to the active channel and is occasionally flooded. Soil profile has alternating bands of deposition and frequently has buried organic horizons.
4	Flood plain (abandoned)	Older, generally frozen portion of a flood plain with a surface layer of ice-rich lowland loess and fine-grained material up to 10 ft thick over granular deposits. Commonly it has tussocks, bogs, and stunted black spruce. Removal of vegetation causes permafrost to recede.
5	Flood plain (other)	Other flood plain/fluvial deposits such as alluvial fan, terrace deposits, mud volcanoes, deltaic, and glacial outwash.
6	Lowland muck	"Re-transported deposits" of fine-grained, organic rich materials moved downslope by slope wash, solifluction, and in some cases by underground erosion. This landform is commonly frozen and contains massive ice. The lowland muck landform can be distinguished from abandoned flood plain in that it must have some slope to this landform.
7	Glacial	Formed in direct contact with glacial ice. Deposits range from unsorted, unstratified, silt, sand, gravel, and boulders, to poorly sorted sand and gravel with some boulders and some local stratification. Examples are moraines, till sheets, drumlins, and compacted till.
8	Lacustrine	Typically fine-grained sediments (silt and clay) that were deposited in both glacial and nonglacial lakes. Lake sediments are generally well stratified into very thin laminations.

Table 7—Landforms (continued)

Code	Class	Description
9	Marine	Any materials that were deposited within saltwater bodies under an ocean and along their margins and composed of very fine-grained to coarse-grained material. Examples are beach spit, bar, and other coarse-grained shallow and inter-tidal deposits.
10	Organic	Decaying plant and animal matter; humus, muck, peat, with or without small amounts of fine-grained sediments (silt and clay). Examples are swamps, bogs, wet sedge fens, and muskegs.
11	Residual	Materials weathered in place from underlying bedrock.
12	Manmade	Deposits or surface materials resulting from human activity, particularly construction and mining.

Table 8—Soil texture

Code	Class[a]	Description
1	Gravel	Rock material. Gravel can range from pea size to boulders. It includes river gravel, which is smooth, to weathered bedrock, which can be chunky or platy.
2	Sand	Particle size 2.0 to 0.05 mm. Individual particles feel gritty when the soil is rubbed between the fingers. Not plastic or sticky when moist.
3	Loam	A mixture of sand, silt, and clay. It is fairly soft with evident graininess.
4	Silt	Particle size 0.05 to 0.002 mm. Feels smooth and powdery when rubbed between the fingers. Not plastic or sticky when moist.
5	Clay	Particle size less than 0.002 mm. Feels smooth, sticky, and plastic when moist. Forms a ribbon when rolled in hand. Forms hard clods when dry.
6	Organic	Decomposing vegetative material. May contain small amounts of mineral soil and small amounts of partially decomposed roots.
7	Ash	Particle size less than 2.0 mm. Volcanic ash is fine rock and mineral particles that are ejected from a volcanic vent. Feels hard and abrasive to the touch.

[a] Classes follow the Natural Resources Conservation Service definitions.

Table 9—Soil moisture

Code	Class	Description
1	Peraquic	Soil is saturated for most of the year when the soil is not frozen. During the driest part of the growing season, water is found above, at, or just below the surface of the mineral soil. Peraquic soil is commonly found in surface organic layers. The soil is extremely poorly drained.
2	Aquic	Soil is saturated during a large part of the year. During the driest part of the year, the water level in the soil may drop below the mineral soil surface but is always within 1 foot of the mineral surface. Thin organic horizons may dry out completely; organic horizons greater than 1 foot may be wet at low levels. The soil is poorly drained. Soil saturation may be due to high groundwater level because of nearby water courses or water perched by underlying permafrost.
3	Subaquic	Soil is saturated during a significant portion of the year. During the growing season, the water level in the soil commonly drops below the surface of the mineral soil. The water table may fluctuate owing to runoff or changes in river level. Organic horizons may dry out; free water is not readily available to plants. The soil is somewhat poorly drained. Typically water is slow moving but may rise rapidly.
4	Perhumid	Soil is well- to moderately well-drained and has an abundant supply of moving well-oxygenated water. Generally the soil has adequate moisture in a portion of the rooting zone during the growing season. Often a distinct root mat occurs immediately above the surface in the zone of free-flowing water. With some exceptions, perhumid soil moisture is found between mid slope and valley floor or on benches and along streams or rivers.
5	Humid	Soil is classified as well-drained with an adequate water supply for growth during a majority of the growing season. Free water is only present during the spring thaw or following extended periods of rain.
6	Subhumid	Soil is dry for a considerable period of the growing season. Typically, subhumid sites occur only on southern exposures, on coarse soil material such as gravels or sands, or on convex slopes such as ridges and upper slopes.
7	Subxeric	Soils are extremely dry for growing conditions. These sites are confined to southern aspects and occasionally thin soils overlying bedrock. Water is a limiting factor for plant growth.
8	Xeric	Soil is dry in all parts of the rooting zone. Xeric soils are only found on south-facing aspects and steep slopes from upper through mid slopes. For most of the growing season, soil moisture is limiting for vegetative growth.

Table 10—Deadwood, charcoal, mineral soil, litter, and tree cover class

Class	Cover on the permanent sample plot
	Percent
0.5	Trace
1	1 to <5
2	5 to <25
3	25 to <50
4	50 to <75
5	75 to <95
6	>95

Tree Records

There are 28 tree attributes. Their names, data types, and units are listed in table 11. Detailed descriptions are given below:

TREE_ID: Unique 5-digit tree number assigned in the database for each tree (linked to plot and TAG_NUMBER).

PSP: PSP number.

TAG_NUMBER: Tag number assigned in the field to each tree.

SPCD: Tree species by number code. See table 12 for details.

DBH: Present diameter measured at 4.5 ft aboveground on the high side of tree (to the nearest 0.01 in).

TLHT: Present total tree height measured from ground to top of live crown (to the nearest foot).

CRLN: Present crown length measured from bottom of live crown to top of live crown (to the nearest foot).

PREVDBH: Diameter at breast height measured at the previous inventory (to the nearest 0.01 in).

PREVTLHT: Total tree height measured at the previous inventory (to the nearest foot).

PREVCRLN: Crown length at the previous inventory measured from bottom of live crown to top of live crown (to the nearest foot).

CRCL: Coded crown class. See table 13 for details.

STAT: Status of each numbered tree. See table 14 for details.

DLO1 to DLO4: Location of the four most prominent visual damages on tree. See table 15 for code details. DLO1 represents the most outstanding damage, and DLO4 the least. Location codes:

0 = No damage

1 = Damage not specified

2 = Tip of tree

3 = Foliage

4 = Limb

5 = Bole, 2 ft and above

6 = Base, below 2 ft

7 = Roots

8 = Leaning or bent tree

9 = Down tree

DSV1 to DSV4: Severity of the four most prominent visual damages on tree. DSV1 represents the most outstanding damage, and DSV4 the least. See table 15 for code details. Severity codes:

0 = Unspecified.

1 = Minor; ≤ 10 percent defect/damage.

2 = Moderate; 11 to 40 percent defect/damage.

3 = Severe; > 40 percent defect/damage.

DTY1 to DTY4: General type of the four most prominent visual damages on tree. DTY1 represents the most outstanding damage, and DTY4 the least. See table 15 for code details.

DSP1 to DSP4: Specific cause and nature of the four most prominent visual damages on tree. DSP1 represents the most outstanding damage, and DSP4 the least. See specific damage codes in table 15.

Table 11—Tree inventory variables

Column	Name	Data type	Value or unit of measure
TREE_ID	Tree ID	Integer	Index
PSP	PSP number	Integer	Index
TAG_NUMBER	Tag number	Integer	Index
SPCD	Species code	Integer	Coded
DBH	Diameter at breast height	Real number	Inches
TLHT	Total height	Real number	Feet
CRLN	Crown length	Real number	Feet
PREVDBH	Diameter at breast height for the previous inventory	Real number	Inches
PREVTLHT	Total height for the previous inventory	Real number	Feet
PREVCRLN	Crown length for the previous inventory	Real number	Feet
CRCL	Crown class	Integer	Coded
STAT	Status	Integer	Coded
DLO1	Damage location 1	Integer	Coded
DSV1	Damage severity 1	Integer	Coded
DTY1	Damage type 1 (general)	Integer	Coded
DSP1	Damage specific 1	Integer	Coded
DLO2	Damage location 2	Integer	Coded
DSV2	Damage severity 2	Integer	Coded
DTY2	Damage type 2 (general)	Integer	Coded
DSP2	Damage specific 2	Integer	Coded
DLO3	Damage location 3	Integer	Coded
DSV3	Damage severity 3	Integer	Coded
DTY3	Damage type 3 (general)	Integer	Coded
DSP3	Damage specific 3	Integer	Coded
DLO4	Damage location 4	Integer	Coded
DSV4	Damage severity 4	Integer	Coded
DTY4	Damage type 4 (general)	Integer	Coded
DSP4	Damage specific 4	Integer	Coded

Table 12—Tree species code

Code	Common name	Scientific name[a]
1	Alaskan birch	*Betula neoalaskana* Sarg.
3	Black cottonwood, balsam poplar	*Populus trichocarpa* Torr. &Gray, *P. balsamifera* L.
4	Quaking aspen	*Populus tremuloides* Michx.
5	White spruce	*Picea glauca* (Moench) Voss
6	Black spruce	*Picea mariana* (Mill.) B.S.P.
7	Tamarack	*Larix laricina* (DuRoi) K.Koch
8	Kenai birch	*Betula kenaica* W.H. Evans

[a] Nomenclature per *Flora of North America north of Mexico*, 1993.

Table 13—Crown class description

Code	Class	Description
0	No estimate	Code 0 is entered if no other entry is present.
1	Dominant	Crown extends above the general canopy layer for the stand. The crown intercepts direct light across the top and along sides of the upper branches. Crown is well developed and large, although usually somewhat crowed along the lower branches. Tree diameter is usually among the largest in the stand.
2	Codominant	Crown within and helping to form the main crown canopy for the stand. Crown intercepts direct sunlight across the top but only at the tips of the upper side branches. The crown is well-developed but of only medium size and crowded at the sides. Tree diameter among the upper range of those present, but not the largest in the stand.
3	Intermediate	Crown extends somewhat into the lower part of the main canopy. The crown intercepts direct sunlight only at a limited area on the top and none at the sides. Crown is narrow and short with limited leaf surface area and a low live-crown ratio. Tree diameter within the lower range of those present but not necessarily the smallest.
4	Suppressed	Crown is entirely below the main canopy and covered by branches of taller trees. No direct sunlight strikes any portion of the crown. The crown is small, often lopsided, flat-topped, and sparse. Tree diameter is among the smallest in the stand. Suppressed trees will probably not respond to release.
5	Understory	Crown is entirely below the main canopy including below intermediate tree crowns. Understory trees are shade-tolerant species and will probably respond to release.
6	Overstory	Tree in an even-aged stand that is substantially older than the average age of the main canopy.
7	Off-site tree	A site tree or buffer strip tree located off the site property. This tree may be measured for site estimates or included in stem maps but excluded from site summaries.

Table 14—Tree status description

Code	Class	Description
0	Live	Tree is alive.
1	Live, cut	Tree is alive but has been cut, such as a tree cut above snow level where the remaining portion of the tree lives.
2	Dead	A tree that is numbered within the site but has died of natural causes. It is counted as a snag.
3	Ingrowth	Tree has grown from regeneration size (≤0.50 inch) to tree size (>0.50 inch) since the last measurement period. Prior to 2002, the theshold of regeneration size was 1.50 inches
4	New tree previously missed	Tree that is too large to be considered ingrowth. It obviously was not tagged/measured as a tree in the previous inventory.
5	Dead, cut	Tree is dead. It was cut by humans.
6	Site tree	An off-plot tree selected to be measured for site estimates.
7	Crop tree	An off-plot tree selected to become a component of a future commercial harvest.
8	New tree, smaller diameter class	In 2002, the forest growth and yield program changed the definition of a tree. Previously a tree had a d.b.h. of >1.50 inches, and a tree ≤1.50 inches in d.b h. was considered regeneration. Since 2002, the threshold of regeneration size has been 0.50 in.
9	Correct measurement	Tree was measured incorrectly during the last measurement period. This year's measurement is correct.
10	Missing number tag	Tree was previously numbered, but numbered tag cannot be found at the base of the tree.
11	Correct tree species	Tree species was incorrectly identified in the previous inventory.
12	Incorrect diameter	Tree d.b h. measurement is extreme/incorrect in this inventory.
13	Incorrect height	Tree height measurement is extreme/incorrect in this inventory.

Table 15—Tree damage code description

Code	Class		Specific cause and nature
0	Unknown or unspecified damage	0	Unknown or unspecified damage
1	Human activity	0	Unknown or unspecified
		1	Logging
		2	Foliage sprays
		3	Bole treatment
		4	Root or soil treatment
		5	Prunning
		6	Peeled bark
		7–9	User defined
2	Crown disease and abnormalities	0	Unknown or unspecified
		1	Unhealthy appearance
		2	Foliage diseases
		3	Broom rust/mistletoe
		4	Dieback
		5	Leaner
		6	Multiple tops
		7	Spruce needle cast
		8–9	User defined

Table 15—Tree damage code description (continued)

Code	Class		Specific cause and nature
3	Bole diseases and abnormalities	0	Unknown or unspecified
		1	Bole rot
		2	Multiple stems and forks
		3	Stem cankers/burls/galls
		4	Sweep or crook
		5	Dead or broken top
		6	Epicormic branching
		7	Fluting
		8	Scare
		9	Layering
4	Root Diseases	0	Unknown or unspecified
		1	Root throw
		2–9	User defined
5	Insects	0	Unknown or unspecified
		1	Defoliators
		2	Bark beetles
		3	Sucking insects
		4	Aphids
		5	Spruce budworm
		6	Leaf roller
		7	Ants
		8	Leaf miner
		9	Ips beetle
6	Mammals and birds	0	Unknown or unspecified
		1	Moose, deer, elk, caribou
		2	Bear
		3	Livestock
		4	Porcupine
		5	Beaver
		6	Hare
		7	Bird
		8–9	User defined
7	Fire	0	Unknown or unspecified
		1	Wild fire
		2	Controlled burn
		3–9	User defined
8	Weather	0	Unknown or unspecified
		1	Wind
		2	Snow/ice
		3	Freeze
		4	Drought
		5	Winter burn
		6–9	User defined
9	Miscellaneous	0–9	User defined

Summary Statistics

Table 16 summarizes the mean, standard deviation, maximum, minimum, and count of all the site data. Summary statistics of all the tree data from the three inventories are shown in tables 17 through 19. Because only a proportion of PSPs have been remeasured, tables 18 and 19 represent fewer PSPs than does table 17.

Table 16—Summary statistics of site attributes

Variable	Unit	Mean[a]	Std[b]	Maximum	Minimum	Count
Elevation	Foot	355	246.96	1,071	0	556
Latitude	Degree	62	4.79	65	0	556
Longitude	Degree	146	11.17	152	0	556
ASPC	Degree	151	109.32	368	0	566
SLOP	Percent	11	12.62	77	0	567
PERM	Coded	4		5	0	566
SLPO	Coded	4		13	1	563
CONT	Coded	2		4	1	566
BDRK	Coded	3		4	0	566
LNFM	Coded	7		11	1	567
SOTXI	Coded	4		6	1	534
SOTXII	Coded	3		7	1	253
SOOR	Inch	457	2,068.43	9,915	0.50	548
SOOi	Inch	1	1.33	12	0	406
SOOe	Inch	2	6.75	135	0	406
SOOa	Inch	127	1,104.72	9,911	0	398
SOMD	Inch	939	2,880.79	9,930	0	525
SOMO	Coded	5		8	0	540
DDWD1	Coded	1		4	0	566
DDWD2	Coded	1		4	0	406
DDWD3	Coded	2		4	1	93
CHAR1	Coded	0		3	0	566
CHAR2	Coded	0		2	0	406
CHAR3	Coded	0		3	0	93
MNSO1	Coded	0		3	0	566
MNSO2	Coded	0		4	0	406
MNSO3	Coded	0		2	0	93
LTER1	Coded	2		6	0	566
LTER2	Coded	3		6	0	406
LTER3	Coded	4		6	1	93
SNAG1		14	17.94	119	0	558
SNAG2		15	22.68	209	0	386
SNAG3		23	20.18	117	0	89

[a] Median if records are discrete or coded.
[b] Standard deviation.

Table 17—Summary statistics of tree records in the first inventory

Variable	Unit	Mean[a]	Std[b]	Maximum	Minimum	Count
DBH	Inch	4	2.77	33.62	0.51	46,027
TLHT	Foot	29	17.12	123	1	42,519
CRLN	Foot	15	10.59	99	1	42,414
CRCL	Coded	3		9	1	46,378
STAT	Coded					0
DLO1	Coded	5		9	1	32,070
DSV1	Coded	2		5	1	32,071
DTY1	Coded	3		8	1	32,062
DSP1	Coded	4		9	1	32,056
DLO2	Coded	5		9	1	13,902
DSV2	Coded	2		8	1	13,897
DTY2	Coded	3		9	1	13,892
DSP2	Coded	4		9	1	13,882
DLO3	Coded	3		8	1	4,369
DSV3	Coded	2		8	1	4,370
DTY3	Coded	3		9	2	4,369
DSP3	Coded	4		9	1	4,367
DLO4	Coded	4		8	1	981
DSV4	Coded	2		8	1	981
DTY4	Coded	3		9	2	981
DSP4	Coded	4		9	1	981

[a] Median if records are discrete or coded.
[b] Standard deviation.

Table 18—Summary statistics of tree records in the second inventory

Variable	Unit	Mean[a]	Std[b]	Maximum	Minimum	Count
DBH	Inch	4	3.05	142	0.27	31,028
TLHT	Foot	31	19.00	118	1	28,914
CRLN	Foot	16	11.63	100	1	28,904
CRCL	Coded	3		44	1	31,453
STAT	Coded	3		11	1	10,010
DLO1	Coded	5		9	1	24,066
DSV1	Coded	2		8	1	24,061
DTY1	Coded	3		9	1	24,069
DSP1	Coded	4		9	1	24,055
DLO2	Coded	5		9	1	12,727
DSV2	Coded	2		6	1	12,724
DTY2	Coded	3		9	1	12,722
DSP2	Coded	4		9	1	12,713
DLO3	Coded	3		8	1	4,744
DSV3	Coded	2		5	1	4,743
DTY3	Coded	4		9	1	4,740
DSP3	Coded	4		9	1	4,735
DLO4	Coded	4		8	1	1,179
DSV4	Coded	2		8	1	1,179
DTY4	Coded	4		6	2	1,176
DSP4	Coded	4		9	1	1,175

[a] Median if records are discrete or coded.
[b] Standard deviation.

Table 19—Summary statistics of tree records in the third inventory

Variable	Unit	Mean[a]	Std[b]	Maximum	Minimum	Count
DBH	Inch	4	3.85	215	0.40	8,247
TLHT	Foot	35	19.89	111	1	7,540
CRLN	Foot	18	12.68	93	1	7,531
CRCL	Coded	3		9	1	8,337
STAT	Coded	3		10	2	3,335
DLO1	Coded	5		9	1	6,548
DSV1	Coded	2		12	1	6,554
DTY1	Coded	3		33	1	6,551
DSP1	Coded	5		9	1	6,526
DLO2	Coded	3		8	1	3,825
DSV2	Coded	1		7	1	3,826
DTY2	Coded	3		13	1	3,822
DSP2	Coded	5		9	1	3,810
DLO3	Coded	3		9	1	1,294
DSV3	Coded	2		8	1	1,298
DTY3	Coded	4		8	1	1,296
DSP3	Coded	5		8	1	1,292
DLO4	Coded	4		8	1	196
DSV4	Coded	2		5	1	196
DTY4	Coded	4		8	2	195
DSP4	Coded	5		8	1	193

[a] Median if records are discrete or coded.
[b] Standard deviation.

Acknowledgments

The publication was funded by the Boreal Ecology Cooperative Research Unit, Pacific Northwest Research Station. We thank Teresa N. Hollingsworth, Thomas A. Hanley, John A. Laurence, and Paul H. Dunn and for their assistance in publication. We also thank Mo Zhou and John Yarie for their useful comments on the manuscript.

The work leading to the CAFI was supported, in part, by the Federal McIntire-Stennis Fund, the University of Alaska Fairbanks School of Natural Resources and Agricultural Sciences, State of Alaska Division of Forestry, and the Natural Resource Fund.

Metric Equivalents

When you know:	Multiply by:	To find:
Inches (in)	2.54	Centimeters (cm)
Feet (ft)	.3048	Meters (m)
Miles (mi)	1.609	Kilometers (km)
Square feet (ft^2)	.0929	Square meters (m^2)
Square feet per acre (ft^2/ac)	.2294	Square meters per hectare (m^2/ha)
Acres (ac)	.4050	Hectares (ha)
Degrees Fahrenheit (°F)	.56(°F - 32)	Degrees Celsius (°C)

Literature Cited

Curtis, R.O. 1983. Procedures for establishing and maintaining permanent plots for silvicultural and yield research. Gen. Tech. Rep. PNW-155. Portland, OR: U.S. Department of Agriculture, Forest Service, Pacific Northwest Forest and Range Experiment Station. 56 p.

Flora of North America Editorial Committee. 1993. Flora of North America north of Mexico. Vol. 2, 3, 7. New York, NY: Oxford University Press.

Helms, J.A. 1998. The dictionary of forestry. Bethesda, MD: Society of American Foresters. 210 p.

Macbeth, G. 2000. Munsell soil color charts. New Windsor, NY: Gretag Macbeth. 31 p.

Schoeneberger, P.J., Wysocki, D.A., Benham, E.C., Broderson,W.D., eds., 2002. Field book for describing and sampling soils, version 2.0. Lincoln, NE: U.S. Department of Agriculture, Natural Resources Conservation Service, National Soil Survey Center.

Van Cleve, K.; Dyrness, C.T. 1983. Introduction and overview of a multidisciplinary research project: the structure and function of a black spruce (*Picea mariana*) forest in relation to other fire-affected taiga ecosystems. Canadian Journal of Forest Research. 13(5): 695–702.

Van Cleve, K.; Oliver, L.; Schlentner, R.; Viereck, L.A.; Dyrness, C.T. 1983. Productivity and nutrient cycling in taiga forest ecosystems. Canadian Journal of Forest Research. 13: 747–766.

Viereck, L.A. and Little, E.L. 1972. Alaska trees and shrubs. Agriculture Handbook No. 410. Washington DC: U.S. Department of Agriculture, Forest Service. 265 p.

Appendix 1: List of Equipment Used to Establish Permanent Sample Plots

GPS unit

Hand-held field computers with shoulder straps

Camera with extra batteries

Laser hypsometer with extra batteries

Laser reflector target

Compass

Clinometer

Convex spherical crown densiometer

Clipboard

100-ft tape (2)

Diameter tapes

Increment borer

Shovel

Regeneration pole

DHB stick (4.5 ft)

Tree data classification sheet

Munsell soil color chart book

Permit from landowner

PSP user's manual

Appendix 2: List of Expendable Supplies Used to Establish Permanent Sample Plots

Pencils

Previous inventory data sheets for remeasurement plots

Blank write-in-the-rain data sheets for site, tree, and regeneration files

Permanent marker pens

Tree core holder tray (2)

Stakes/corner posts (15 per site)

Numbered tags

Pins for numbered tags

Flagging

Lumber crayon

Paint sticks

Rubber gloves

Toilet paper

Bug spray

Bear spray

Zip-lock bags for vegetation samples

Permit from landowner to enter land

Emergency contact phone numbers

Site coordinates

Glossary[1]

acre—A unit of land containing 43,560 ft^2 of area. 0.4 ha.

alluvial fan—A fan-shaped mass of sediment, especially silt, sand, gravel, and boulders, deposited by a river when its flow is suddenly slowed. Alluvial fans typically form where a river pours out from a steep valley through mountains onto a flat plain. Unlike deltas, they are not deposited into a body of standing water.

aphids—members of the *Homoptera* family. See sap-sucking insects.

aspect—A position facing a particular direction usually expressed as a compass direction in degrees. The direction land faces.

bark—The outer layer of a tree stem outside the vascular cambium derived from cell division.

bark beetle—Member of the family Scolytidae and the genera: *Dendroctonus*, *Ips*, or *Scolytus*. Adults and larvae tunnel in the cambial region of trees and can cause severe damage. Some are carriers of disease.

bedrock—The solid rock that underlies the soil and other unconsolidated material that is exposed at the earth's surface.

bole—The trunk or main stem of a tree.

borderline tree—A tree that is difficult to judge as being in or out of a site because it is located close to the PSP border.

boustrophedonic numbering—A system of numbering alternate lines in opposite directions; numbering one line from right to left and the next line from left to right.

breast height—4.5 ft (137 cm) above ground. A standard location for measurement of tree diameter.

broom rust—This fungus, *Chrysomyxa arctostaphyli*, infects spruce trees and causes dense perennial witches' brooms. It causes reduced growth, bole deformation, and an entry court for decay fungi.

browse/browsing—Any woody vegetation consumed or fit for consumption by livestock or wild animals; mainly ungulates. To forage or graze on the buds, stems, and leaves of woody growth.

budworm—A larva of the family Tortricidae that feed on and in buds and young shoots.

burl—Globe-shaped woody growth on boles or branches of both conifers and hardwoods. The cause of burls is not known, but infection by bacteria, viruses, or mycoplasms, and insects is suspected.

canker—A localized usually well-defined sunken or swollen necrotic lesion to stem, branch, or root; caused by disease or insects.

conifer—A cone-bearing tree; gymnosperm.

canopy—The cover of foliage formed by tree crowns.

cardinal direction—One of the four principal directions on a compass: 0° or 360°, north; 90°, east; 180°, south; and 270°, west.

chroma—A relative purity, strength, or saturation of a soil color; directly related to the dominance of the determining wavelength of the light and inversely related to grayness of soil. Chroma is one of three variables of color used to describe soils.

clinometer—An instrument for measuring angles of elevation or depression.

codominant tree—Tree whose crown receives full light from above and little from the sides. These crowns usually form the general level of the upper canopy.

conk—The visible fruiting body of a wood-destroying fungus, which projects from the trunk, roots, or other tree parts. They commonly indicate the presence of rot in the underlying wood.

contour—The general form of the land surface, from straight to undulating.

controlled burn/prescribed burn—A deliberate burning of wildland fuels in either their natural or a modified state. Planned resource management objectives can be attained by controlling the timing, intensity, and size of burns.

crown—The part of a tree or woody plant bearing live branches and foliage.

crown base—The point of attachment of the lowest live whorl on the bole of a tree.

crown class—The relative position of the tree crown with respect to the competing vegetation around it. Crown class for each tree is judged in the context of its immediate environment—those trees or shrubs that are competing for sunlight with the subject tree. In this manual, crown class categories include codominant, dominant intermediate, overstory, suppressed, and understory.

crown cover—The ground area covered by the crowns of trees and other woody vegetation as delimited by the vertical projection of crown perimeters. It is expressed as a class of crown cover.

crown length—Live crown of a standing tree. The vertical distance from the tip of the leader to the base of the live crown, measured to the lowest live whorl without regard for branch droop.

crook—An abrupt bend or curvature in the bole of a tree. A crook is a sound-cull deduction from gross merchantable volume.

database—A collection of data stored in a systematic manner such that the data can be readily retrieved, modified, and manipulated to produce information.

dead tree—A tree having no viable meristematic tissue but self-supporting and with the upper bole standing (not in contact with the surface).

densiometer—An instrument for determining optical density. In forestry applications, a calibrated spherical crown densiometer determines percentage of crown cover.

diameter at breast height (d.b.h.)—A measure of the tree bole, (4.5 ft or 137 cm) above ground outside the bark and perpendicular to the tree bole.

diameter tape—A measure specifically graduated so that tree diameter can be read directly from the tape when placed around a tree stem.

disease—A harmful deviation from normal function of physiological processes; pathogenic or abiotic in origin.

dominant tree—Tree whose crown receives full light from above and partial light from the sides. Crown extends above the general level of the upper canopy.

drumlin—An elongated or oval hill formed by glacial sediments.

edge effect—The modified environmental conditions or habitat along the margins (edges) of forest stands.

epicormic branching—A shoot arising spontaneously from a dormant bud on the stem or branch of a woody plant, often following exposure to increased light.

fern—A nonwoody vascular plant.

flagging—Colored plastic or paper ribbon attached to trees, bushes, or stakes to mark boundaries or to make stakes and other objects more visible.

fluting—Swelling of a tree bole owing to disturbances or rapid growth.

flood plain—The level or nearly level land with alluvial soils on either or both sides of a stream or river.

abandoned flood plain—Land in a flood plain that is no longer subject to periodic flooding.

active flood plain—Land that commonly has newly deposited fluvial sediments and debris moved by floodwaters.

forest—An ecosystem characterized by a more-or-less dense and extensive tree cover, often consisting of stands varying in characteristics such as species composition, structure, age class, and associated processes, and commonly including meadows, streams, fish, and wildlife.

gall—A pronounced swelling or abnormal growth, usually localized, of greatly modified tissue structure arising on plants in response to irritation by a foreign organism (commonly an insect or pathogen).

geographic information system (GIS)—An organized collection of computer hardware, software, geographic and descriptive data, and procedures designed to efficiently capture, store, update, manipulate, analyze, report, and display forms of geographically referenced information and descriptive information.

global positioning system (GPS)—A hand-held, satellite-based navigational device that records x, y, z coordinates and other data allowing users to determine their location on or near the surface of the Earth.

grass—A nonwoody vascular plant that is a member of the Poaceae family.

growth model—A set of relationships, usually expressed as equations and embodied in a computer program, that estimates future stand development given initial stand conditions and a specified management regime. Growth and yield models are used to generate managed-stand yield tables, predict future stand conditions for management planning, update inventories, and compare predicted results of alternative possible management regimes.

herbs—Nonwoody vascular plants such as grasses, grasslike plants, and forbs.

horizon, soil—A layer of soil approximately parallel to the land surface and differing from adjacent genetically related layers in physical, chemical, or biological properties or characteristics such as color, texture, or consistency. Soil taxonomy identifies horizons in a systematic manner.

hue—A measure of chromatic composition of light that reaches the eye. Hue is one of three variables of color used to describe soils.

humus (organic matter, soil)—Black or brown organic material of complex composition that is the end product of microbial breakdown of plant and animal residue under or on the soil surface.

hypsometer—Any instrument for measuring the height of an object (trees) from observations taken at some distance from the object.

increment borer—An auger-like instrument with a hollow bit and an extractor used to extract thin radial cylinders of wood (increment cores) from trees having annual growth rings, to determine diameter increment or age.

insect—A member of the class Insecta characterized by a body segmented into three distinct regions. Often considered a forest pest.

ingrowth tree—A tree that has grown past a diameter or height threshold on a site since previous inventory to become a measurement tree.

intermediate tree—Tree whose crown receives little direct light from above and none from the sides. Crowns are below or extend into the general level of the upper canopy.

lacustrine—Relating to a lake or a standing body of water.

landform—The physical process that formed the topographic features of an area.

layering—A form of vegetative reproduction in which an intact branch develops roots as the result of contact with soil or other growing media.

leaf miner—Various species of leaf miner attack birch, quaking aspen, balsam poplar/black cottonwood, and numerous shrubs of the genera *Alnus* and *Salix*. Larvae enter the leaf and mine between the epidermal layers reducing photosynthetic area. Heavy repeated attacks could reduce tree growth and cause branch dieback.

leaf roller—Numerous species of the genus *Epinotia*, which attack birch, willow, alder, aspen, and balsam poplar. Larvae roll leaves that are skeletonized; these leaves turn brown and drop prematurely. Branch dieback and tree mortality rarely occurs.

leaning tree—The deflection of a tree stem from a vertical line passing through the center of the base and top of the main stem.

lichen—A nonvascular composite organism formed from the symbiotic association of a true fungus and an alga.

litter—The surface layer of a forest floor that is not in an advanced stage of decomposition; usually consisting of freshly fallen leaves, needles, stems, twigs, bark, and fruits.

live crown length—The straight-line distance measured parallel to the main bole of a tree from the top of the live crown to the base of the live crown.

live tree—A tree having viable meristematic tissue and roots in contact with mineral soil.

loam—A soil texture class containing roughly equal amounts of sand, silt, and clay.

loess—Material transported and deposited by wind and consisting of predominantly silt-sized particles.

meridian—A line running vertically from the North Pole to the South Pole along which all locations have the same longitude. The prime meridian, 0°, runs through Greenwich, England; both east and west longitudes range from 0° to 180° relative to the prime meridian.

mesoscale—Of intermediate size on the landscape.

mineral soil—A soil consisting predominantly of, and having its properties determined predominantly by, mineral matter.

Munsell color system—A system that specifies the relative degrees of the three variables of color: hue, value, and chroma.

modeling—A simplified framework designed to illustrate complex processes.

moraine—An accumulation of glacial drift (sediments and rocks) that forms topographic features built chiefly by direct glacial movement. Moraines often develop parallel to (lateral moraine) or perpendicular to (terminal moraines) glaciers as they move.

moss—Short, soft nonvascular plants of the division Bryophyta.

native species—An indigenous species that is normally found as part of a particular ecosystem.

needle/leaf cast—Any untimely shedding of foliage, most often caused by a fungus.

nonvascular plant—Relating to plants not having phloem- and xylem-conducting elements, such as bryophytes.

organic soil—Vegetative and animal matter almost completely decomposed. Organic soil may contain other material, but at least 75 percent must be organic material.

overstory tree—A tree that has survived from the previous stand and is usually larger or older than trees that originated as part of the present stand.

parent material—The unconsolidated and more-or-less chemically weathered mineral or organic matter from which the soil horizons are developed.

pedogenic—The process whereby soil is formed from parent material, i.e., rocks. Any process related to soil formation.

permafrost—Soil that has had a temperature below freezing for 2 or more years; perennially frozen soil.

permanent sample plot (PSP)—Field plots used in forest research. A system of plots established and periodically remeasured to sample forest conditions and provide long-term data. In this system it is a 0.1-ac square with 66-ft sides.

pruning—The removal of side branches or multiple leaders from a standing tree. Dead or live foliage is cut flush to the stem.

regeneration—A young stand of trees smaller than commercial timber or the understory tree component of a multistoried stand designated as seedlings and saplings. The established progeny from a parent plant.

rock—Relatively hard, naturally formed mineral or petrified matter greater than 0.75 inch in diameter appearing on or near the soil surface as small to large fragments or as relatively large bodies, cliffs, outcrops, or peaks.

rot—Decomposition of wood by fungi or bacteria; decay.

sample—A part of a population consisting of one or more sampling units selected and examined as representative of the whole.

sample plot—An area of land chosen as representative of a much larger area.

sap-sucking insects—In Alaska, mostly aphids that attack both conifers and hardwoods. Trees are injured in two ways: sap sucking reduces the food supply and water to the tree, which reduces growth, and it creates an entry point for secondary insects and fungal disease. Identified by enlarged growth, galls, leaf curling, bleaching, or yellowing foliage.

sapling—A tree whose stem is greater that 4.5 ft in height and less than 0.51 in d.b.h.

seedling—A tree whose stem is less than 0.51 in d.b.h. and less than 4.5 ft in height and has root contact with mineral soil.

seed—The ripened ovule of a plant containing an embryo, seed coat, and nutritive tissue.

shrub—A woody perennial plant differing from a perennial herb in its persistent and woody stem, and differing from a tree in its lower stature and general absence of a well-defined main stem.

site—An experimental unit to which a treatment is randomly assigned.

site index—A species-specific measure of actual or potential forest productivity expressed in terms of the average height of dominant and/or codominant trees at a specified base age.

site tree—A normally formed live tree in the dominant or codominant crown class. A site tree may have minor damage but can only have minor visible defect, and no evidence of suppression. Site trees are used to determine the site index.

slope—A measure of deviation of the surface elevation over distance, expressed in degrees or percentage.

slope position—The position of a site in relation to the surrounding topography.

snag—A standing dead tree in the current inventory. A snag must be large enough to be a tree (>0.50 in d.b.h. and 4.5 ft in height) and not severed from its rootstock or uprooted.

solifluction—The slow creeping of saturated soil downslope. This usually occurs in regions of perennial cold climate.

soil—The unconsolidated mineral or organic material on the immediate surface of the earth that serves as the natural medium for the growth of land plants.

soil color—The color of soil horizons determined from the Munsell soil color chart. The notation for color consists of separate notations for hue, value, and chroma, which are combined in that order to form a color designation.

soil moisture—The amount of water in the soil, which is indicative of the general soil drainage.

soil texture—A characteristic consistency of soil determined by relative proportions of various soil fractions: sand, silt, clay, and rock fragments.

species—The main category of taxonomic classification into which genera are subdivided comprising a group of similar interbreeding individuals sharing a common morphology, physiology, and reproductive process. A numeric code identifies each tree species in the CAFI database.

stand—A contiguous group of trees sufficiently uniform in age-class distribution, composition, and structure and growing on a site of sufficiently uniform quality to be a distinguishable unit.

stand age—The mean age of a forest stand that best characterizes the stand. Stands can be even-aged or uneven-aged.

stem—The principal axis of a plant from which buds and shoots develop; stems may be of any age or diameter.

stump—The basal portion of a tree remaining in contact with the soil.

suppressed tree—A tree having its crown in the lower layer of the canopy and whose leading shoot is not free to grow. The crown receives no direct sunlight.

sweep—A broad arc in a bole of a tree or log.

talus—A slope landform typically covered by coarse rock debris forming a more-or-less continuous layer that may or may not be covered by organic material.

tree—A woody perennial plant, typically large, with a single well-defined stem carrying a more-or-less definite crown. In the CAFI database, a tree has a d.b.h. of at least 0.51 in and is greater than 4.5 ft in height.

understory—All forest vegetation growing under an overstory.

value—The degree of lightness or darkness of a soil color in relation to a neutral gray scale extending from black to white. Value is one of three variables of color used to describe soils.

vascular—Relating to plants having phloem- and xylem-conducting elements.

vegetation code—Coding system used to identify vegetative items in this survey

weathering—All physical and chemical changes produced in rocks at or near the earth's surface by atmospheric agents.

windthrow/root throw/blowdown—Tree or trees felled or broken off by wind.

winter burn—The desiccation of foliage and twigs by dry winds at times when water conduction is restricted by frozen plant tissue. Foliage turns brown and dieback of twigs can occur.

xeric—Pertaining to sites or habitats characterized by decidedly dry conditions.

---

[1] Definitions are from *The Dictionary of Forestry* (Helms 1998).